I Never Saw Another Butterfly

A Musical in Two Acts

Book and Lyrics by
JOSEPH ROBINETTE

Music by
E.A. ALEXANDER

Based upon the play by
CELESTE RASPANTI

Dramatic Publishing
Woodstock, Illinois • England • Australia • New Zealand

IMPORTANT BILLING AND CREDIT REQUIREMENTS

All producers of the musical *must* give credit to Celeste Raspanti as the author of the play and to Joseph Robinette and E.A. Alexander as the author and composer of the musical in all programs distributed in connection with performances of the musical and in all instances in which the title of the musical appears for purposes of advertising, publicizing or otherwise exploiting the musical and/or a production. The names of Celeste Raspanti, Joseph Robinette and E.A. Alexander *must* also appear on a separate line, on which no other name appears, immediately following the title, and *must* appear in size of type not less than fifty percent (50%) the size of the title type. Biographical information on Celeste Raspanti, Joseph Robinette and E.A. Alexander, if included in the playbook, may be used in all programs. *In all programs this notice must appear:*

"Produced by special arrangement with
THE DRAMATIC PUBLISHING COMPANY of Woodstock, Illinois"

*** NOTICE ***

The amateur and stock acting rights to this work are controlled exclusively by THE DRAMATIC PUBLISHING COMPANY without whose permission in writing no performance of it may be given. Royalty must be paid every time a play is performed whether or not it is presented for profit and whether or not admission is charged. A play is performed any time it is acted before an audience. Current royalty rates, applications and restrictions may be found at our Web site: www.dramaticpublishing.com, or we may be contacted by mail at: DRAMATIC PUBLISHING COMPANY, 311 Washington St., Woodstock IL 60098.

COPYRIGHT LAW GIVES THE AUTHOR OR THE AUTHOR'S AGENT THE EXCLUSIVE RIGHT TO MAKE COPIES. This law provides authors with a fair return for their creative efforts. Authors earn their living from the royalties they receive from book sales and from the performance of their work. Conscientious observance of copyright law is not only ethical, it encourages authors to continue their creative work. This work is fully protected by copyright. No alterations, deletions or substitutions may be made in the work without the prior written consent of the publisher. No part of this work may be reproduced or transmitted in any form or by any means, electronic or mechanical, including photocopy, recording, videotape, film, or any information storage and retrieval system, without permission in writing from the publisher. It may not be performed either by professionals or amateurs without payment of royalty. All rights, including, but not limited to, the professional, motion picture, radio, television, videotape, foreign language, tabloid, recitation, lecturing, publication and reading, are reserved.

©MMVII
Book and lyrics by JOSEPH ROBINETTE
Music by E.A. ALEXANDER
Based on the play by CELESTE RASPANTI

Printed in the United States of America
All Rights Reserved
(I NEVER SAW ANOTHER BUTTERFLY)

ISBN: 978-1-58342-411-7

INTRODUCTORY NOTES

From 1942 to 1945 over 15,000 Jewish children passed through Terezin, a former military garrison set up as a ghetto. It soon became a station, a stopping-off place, for hundreds of thousands on their way to the gas chambers of Auschwitz. When Terezin was liberated in May 1945, only about one hundred children were alive to return to what was left of their lives, their homes and families. The story of those years at Terezin remains in drawings and poems collected and published in the book, *I Never Saw Another Butterfly*.

The appendix to *I Never Saw Another Butterfly* briefly notes the names, the dates of their birth and transportation to Terezin. For most of the children whose work appears in the book, the brief biography ends, "perished at Auschwitz..." But one child, Raja Englanderova, "after the liberation, returned to Prague." This musical—based on the play by Celeste Raspanti who also wrote these notes—is an imaginative creation of Raja's story from documentary materials: poems, diaries, letters, journals, drawings and pictures.

I Never Saw Another Butterfly

A Musical in Two Acts
For a cast of 11* – 21 (more, if desired)

FULL CAST (8m, 5w, 8 children [flexible])

RAJA ENGLANDEROVA	from Terezin
FATHER	her father
MOTHER	her mother
PAVEL	her brother
IRCA	Pavel's fiancee
IRENA SYNKOVA	a teacher
RENKA	her assistant
HONZA	a friend of Raja
RABBI	a spiritual leader
1ST CHILD	
2ND CHILD	
3RD CHILD	
4TH CHILD	children of Terezin
5TH CHILD	
6TH CHILD	
7TH CHILD	
8TH CHILD	
1ST OFFICIAL	German officials
2ND OFFICIAL	
1ST SOLDIER	German soldiers
2ND SOLDIER	
OFFSTAGE VOICES	

TIME: 1942 – 1945.
PLACE: Terezin (and Prague), Czechoslovakia.

* See following page for small cast.

SUGGESTED DOUBLING FOR SMALL CAST (3m, 4w and 4 children)

1ST MAN	1ST Official, Pavel, 1ST Soldier
2ND MAN	2ND Official, Father, 2ND Soldier
3RD MAN	Honza, Rabbi
1ST WOMAN	Raja
2ND WOMAN	Renka, Irca
3RD WOMAN	Irena
4TH WOMAN	Mother
1ST CHILD	1ST and 5TH Children
2ND CHILD	2ND and 6TH Children
3RD CHILD	3RD and 7TH Children
4TH CHILD	4TH and 8TH Children
OFFSTAGE VOICES	

(If desired, the actors—including the taller children—when available—may don capes and shawls and appear in crowd scenes and/or the wedding scene.)

MUSICAL NUMBERS

ACT ONE

1. "Terezin"..................... Raja and Company
2. "We'll Stick Together" .... Irena, Renka and Children
3. "The Rules" (spoken over music).. 1ST and 2ND Soldiers
4. "Do the Best With What You've Got" ... Irena, Renka and Children
5. "Welcome Shabbat"... Mother, Father, Raja and Pavel
6. "You Don't Know..."............. Honza and Raja
7. "When I Go Home".................... Children

ACT TWO

8. "Curfew".................. 1ST and 2ND Soldiers
9. "The Gift" .... Raja and Honza
10. "Wedding Psalm"....... Rabbi, Irca, Pavel and Guests
11. "Ludvik" .... Children and Honza
12. "Reprise: You Don't Know..." ...... Raja and Honza
13. "I Leave You These" ...... Irena, Raja and Company
14. "Bows and Reprise: Ludvik"............. Company

ACT ONE

(An open stage with various levels and steps. The several different scenes are suggested by simple props brought on and off by the ACTORS. Modest backdrops and/or projections may be used to enhance the locales.

Before the curtain opens, RAJA, a young woman, is discovered in a softly lighted area at DR. She is silent for a moment, then speaks directly to the audience.)

RAJA. My name—is Raja… I was born in Prague… I am a Jew… And I survived Terezin.

(She exits as the curtain opens. In dim lighting, perhaps accompanied by a light mist or fog, the ACTORS—except for those playing RAJA and the two OFFICIALS—enter as they sing and stand at various points about the stage, perhaps forming a semicircle.)

(SONG #1: "TEREZIN")

GROUP 1.
TEREZIN, TEREZIN, TEREZIN, TEREZIN, TEREZIN, TEREZIN.

GROUP 2.
> **TEREZIN, TEREZIN, TEREZIN, TEREZIN.**

GROUP 3.
> **TEREZIN.**

ALL.
> **IT WAS A TOWN IN THE MIDST OF A LAND MOST BEAUTIFUL**

GROUP 1.
> **RIVERS GENTLY FLOWING, FLOWERS FREELY GROWING.**
> **SONGBIRDS CALLING, COVERED WITH DEW 'NEATH MOUNTAINS SO BLUE AND BUTTERFLIES.**
> **BUTTERFLIES, BUTTERFLIES, BUTTERFLIES.**

GROUP 2.
> **RIVERS FLOWING. FLOWERS GROWING.**
> **MEADOWS SPRAWLING, COVERED WITH DEW**
> **AH, AH, AH, BUTTERFLIES.**

GROUP 3.
> **RIVERS FLOWING, FLOWERS GROWING,**
> **'NEATH MOUNTAINS SO BLUE.**
> **BUTTERFLIES, BUTTERFLIES, BUTTERFLIES, BUTTERFLIES.**

ALL.
> **THERE ALWAYS SEEMED TO BE BUTTERFLIES**

Act I   I NEVER SAW ANOTHER BUTTERFLY

GROUP 1.
>**DOTTING THE SKIES WITH YELLOW AND GOLD AND RED AND BROWN**

GROUP 2 & 3.
>**BUTTERFLIES**

ALL.
>**DARTING PLAYFULLY ABOVE THE TOWN OF TEREZIN**

GROUP 1.
>**IT WAS A TOWN IN THE MIDST OF A LAND MOST BEAUTIFUL...**

GROUP 2 & 3.
>**TEREZIN, TERERZIN, TEREZIN, AH...**

GROUP 1 & 2.
>**UNTIL, UNTIL, UNTIL, UNTIL, UNTIL...**

GROUP 3.
>**AH...**

(Two GERMAN OFFICIALS enter.)

1ST OFFICIAL. I think you have found the perfect place, Herr Muller. High walls, deep moats, narrow streets. And in such a lovely setting.
2ND OFFICIAL. A little jewel in Czechoslovakia's crown.
1ST OFFICIAL. And what do they call this town?

2ND OFFICIAL. Terezin. Built by the emperor Joseph over a hundred and fifty years ago. He named it for his mother, Maria Terese.

1ST OFFICIAL. I think it will make our leader happy, this Terezin.

2ND OFFICIAL. We have followed his orders to the letter. *(He takes out a folded piece of paper and reads.)* "...a place which we can turn into a model ghetto inhabited by Jews. A village we can proudly display to the world if it becomes suspicious of our...other business." The Jews will come here willingly. They are aware of the dangers in their current surroundings.

1ST OFFICIAL. We will attract the best and the brightest to show to the world.

2ND OFFICIAL. But we must also make room for a few of the poor and the sick.

1ST OFFICIAL. Indeed. After all, it *is* to be a *model* ghetto.

2ND OFFICIAL *(again reading from the paper)*. "...a gift to the Jews from the Fuhrer." *(He puts the paper away.)* While he does *his* other business.

1ST OFFICIAL *(saluting)*. Heil, Hitler.

2ND OFFICIAL *(saluting)*. Heil, Hitler.

(They exit.)

ALL *(singing)*.
    TEREZIN, TEREZIN, TEREZIN, TEREZIN.
    IT WAS A TOWN IN THE MIDST OF A LAND
    MOST BEAUTIFUL...UNTIL—

Act I I NEVER SAW ANOTHER BUTTERFLY 13

GROUP 2 & 1 *(alternately)*.
   UNTIL, UNTIL, UNTIL,
   UNTIL, UNTIL, UNTIL,
   UNTIL, UNTIL, UNTIL.

GROUP 3.
AH...

(RAJA reenters.)

RAJA *(speaking)*.
My name is Raja. I was born in
Prague. I am a Jew and I
survived Terezin. But many others
were not as fortunate.

GROUP 1, 2 and 3.
AH, AH, AH...

ACTORS *(speaking in turn)*. Zuzana Winterova,
   11 years old—perished at Auschwitz,
   October 4, 1944... Gabriela Freiova,
   10 years old—perished at Auschwitz,
   May 18, 1944... Frantizek Brozan,
   14 years old—perished at Auschwitz,
   December 15, 1943... Eva Bulova,
   15 years old—perished at Auschwitz,
   October 4, 1944...

(The VOICES begin to fade.)

ALL.

Liana Franklova, 13 years old—
perished at Auschwitz, October
19, 1944... Alfred Weiskopf,
16 years old—perished at
Auschwitz, December 18, 1944...

TEREZIN, TEREZIN,

TEREZIN, TEREZIN,

TEREZIN, TEREZIN.

ALL *(except RAJA singing)*.
>   **IT WAS A TOWN IN THE MIDST OF A LAND MOST BEAUTIFUL.**

SOLO 1.
>   **RIVERS GENTLY FLOWING—**

RAJA *(speaking)*.	ALL *(singing)*.
And there were others.	**AH...**
	SOLO 2. **FLOWERS FREELY GROWING**
My mother, my father...	ALL. **AH—**
	SOLO 3. **SONGBIRDS CALLING,**
	SOLO 4. **MEADOWS SPRAWLING,**
My brother, my aunt, my friends. They are all gone.	ALL. **AH...**
	SOLO 5. **COVERED WITH DEW. 'NEATH MOUNTAINS SO BLUE.**
And I am all alone.	

Act I   I NEVER SAW ANOTHER BUTTERFLY   15

                                      GROUP 1.
                                      AND BUTTERFLIES,

But that is not important.   GROUP 2.
                                      AH…

                                      GROUP 3.
                                      BUTTERFLIES,
                                      BUTTERFLIES.

Only one thing is important…   GROUP 2.
                                      AH—

                                      GROUP 3.
                                      BUTTERFLIES.

                                    GROUP 1.
                                    BUTTERFLIES.

                                    GROUP 2.
                                    AH—

                                    GROUP 3.
                                    BUTTERFLIES.

I am a Jew, and I survived.
                                    ALL.
                                    BUTTERFLIES.

I survived!

(ALL except RAJA exit as a distant train whistle is heard, followed by the low cadence of a beating drum.)

RAJA. In March 1939, Nazi Germany armed forces entered Prague. December 1939, Jewish children were no longer allowed to attend state elementary schools. June 1940, the concentration camp at Auschwitz was established. September 1941, mass deportation of Jews began. October 1941, the first transports left Prague for Terezin. *(A nearer train whistle is heard.)* Among them were children...many children. I was one of them.

(She exits as the screeching brakes of a train are heard.)

STATIONMASTER'S VOICE *(from offstage)*. Train from Prague now arriving. Stand to the back of the platform please. Children will disembark first, followed by women and then men. *(A final train whistle is heard.)* Welcome to Terezin.

(Offstage VOICES of the PASSENGERS are heard, then fade as RENKA, a young woman in her twenties, enters holding the hands of two CHILDREN who carry bags or small suitcases. Other CHILDREN with modest luggage follow behind. They appear somewhat uncertain, even frightened, of their new surroundings.)

RENKA *(calling out)*. Irena, Irena Synkova—it's Renka...

(IRENA, a bit older than RENKA, enters holding a sheaf of odd-sized papers.)

IRENA. Ah...more children have arrived.
RENKA. Nearly four hundred this time.
IRENA. Later, when the workers return—and the older children—we'll make room for this new group in the barracks. Each one must have a place.

Act I I NEVER SAW ANOTHER BUTTERFLY 17

RENKA. And tomorrow, when another trainload arrives?

IRENA. We'll find places for them as well. *And* we'll make room for them in the school. They must start living again.

1ST CHILD. There is a school here?

IRENA. Yes. It won't look like the one you went to. It won't be as nice. But we will learn—and also have fun. I will be your teacher. And Miss Renka will be my helper.

RENKA. We are fortunate the authorities allowed you to establish a school—of any kind.

IRENA. They had little choice. I asked them what outsiders would think when they visited this— *(somewhat sarcastically)* —"model ghetto" and found no school.

2ND CHILD. I want to go back home to my own school.

IRENA. Of course you do. But for now, we'll be here.

3RD CHILD. I don't think I like it here.

IRENA. But you just arrived.

RENKA. You'll get used to it in time.

4TH CHILD. I'm afraid of this place.

IRENA. You're not afraid of me, are you?

4TH CHILD. No.

RENKA. Or me?

4TH CHILD. No.

IRENA *(pointing to another child)*. Or him?

4TH CHILD. No.

RENKA *(pointing to another child)*. Or her?

4TH CHILD *(almost laughing, despite himself)*. No.

5TH CHILD. Or me?

4TH CHILD. No.

6TH CHILD. Or me?

CHILDREN *(each in turn, giggling)*. Or me? Or me? Or me? Or me?

4TH CHILD *(laughing with the others)*. No. No. No. No.

IRENA. There…you see. A place is just a place. But it's the people who make a place what it is. And if the people are always there to help each other, there's no need to be afraid.

(SONG #2: "WE'LL STICK TOGETHER")

IRENA *(singing)*.
> **WE'LL STICK TOGETHER LIKE BIRDS OF A FEATHER,**
> **SO WE CAN WEATHER ANY STORM THAT COMES.**
> **WE HAVE EACH OTHER, WE'LL CARE FOR ONE ANOTHER**
> **LIKE THE VERY, VERY BEST OF CHUMS.**

(Speaking.)
Get into pairs, and I'll show you what I mean.
(Singing to 1ST CHILD.)
> **IF YOU SHOULD FALL IN A HOLE, JUST SHOUT.**

1ST CHILD *(playing along, speaking)*. Oh, no!

IRENA *(singing)*.
> **AND I'LL BE THERE TO HELP YOU OUT.**

(She performs the actions—as all subsequent actions will be performed—then goes to 2ND CHILD.)
> **IF YOU'RE HAVING A DREARY DAY—**

2ND CHILD *(speaking)*. I'm lonesome.

Act I   I NEVER SAW ANOTHER BUTTERFLY   19

IRENA *(singing)*.
   —I'LL COME OVER, AND WE CAN PLAY.

(They play a quick game of patty-cake as IRENA turns to the OTHERS and speaks.)

Okay, who's next?

3RD CHILD *(turning to the 4TH CHILD, singing)*.
   IF YOU'RE EVER STUCK IN A TREE—

4TH CHILD *(speaking)*. I'm caught!

3RD CHILD *(singing)*.
   —I'LL BE THE ONE TO SET YOU FREE.

5TH CHILD.
   IF YOU'RE HAVING A SCARY DREAM—

6TH CHILD *(speaking)*. Help!

5TH CHILD *(singing)*.
   —I'LL BE THERE TO HELP YOU SCREAM.

(She and the 6TH CHILD scream.)

3RD & 5TH CHILDREN *(singing to 4TH and 6TH CHILDREN respectively)*.
   I'LL BE THERE FOR YOU
   ANYTIME YOU WANT ME TO.

4TH & 6TH CHILDREN *(to 3RD and 5TH CHILDREN respectively)*.
>   I'LL BE THERE FOR YOU.
>   I'LL STICK TO YOU LIKE GLUE.

3RD, 4TH, 5TH & 6TH CHILDREN.
>   I'LL BE THERE FOR YOU.
>   WE'LL BE PARTNERS THROUGH AND
>   THROUGH.

7TH CHILD *(to 8TH CHILD)*.
>   IF YOU THINK THERE'S A MONSTER IN YOUR
>   CLOSET—

8TH CHILD *(speaking)*. It's over there!

7TH CHILD *(singing)*.
>   —JUST LET ME GET MY PAWS UPON IT.

1ST CHILD.
>   IF YOU'RE AFRAID OF THE DARK AT NIGHT—

2ND CHILD *(speaking)*. I'm scared!

1ST CHILD *(singing)*.
>   —I'LL BE THERE TO TURN ON THE LIGHT.

RENKA *(to the CHILDREN)*.
>   IF YOU'RE HUNGRY AND NEED TO BE FED—

CHILDREN *(speaking)*. We're starved!

RENKA *(singing)*.
>—I'LL BE THERE WITH BUTTER AND BREAD.

CHILDREN *(speaking)*. Yum!

IRENA & RENKA *(to the CHILDREN, singing)*.
> **IF YOU'RE IN A SINKING BOAT—**

CHILDREN *(speaking)*. Glub! Glub! Glub!

IRENA & RENKA *(singing)*.
> —**WE'LL BE THERE TO HELP YOU FLOAT.**
>
> **WE'LL BE THERE FOR YOU**
> **ANYTIME YOU WANT US TO.**
> **WE'LL BE THERE FOR YOU.**
> **WE'LL STICK TO YOU LIKE GLUE.**
> **WE'LL BE THERE FOR YOU.**
> **WE'LL BE PARTNERS THROUGH AND THROUGH.**

CHILDREN.
> **WE'LL STICK TOGETHER LIKE BIRDS OF A FEATHER,**
> **SO WE CAN WEATHER ANY STORM THAT COMES.**
> **WE HAVE EACH OTHER, WE'LL CARE FOR ONE ANOTHER**
> **LIKE THE VERY, VERY BEST**

IRENA & 1ST GROUP *(FOUR CHILDREN)*.
> —**OF CHUMS—**

RENKA & 2ND GROUP *(FOUR CHILDREN)*.
   —OF CHUMS—

IRENA & 1ST GROUP.
   —AND MATES—

RENKA & 2ND GROUP.
   —AND MATES—

IRENA & 1ST GROUP.
   —AND PALS—

RENKA & 2ND GROUP.
   —AND PALS—

IRENA & 1ST GROUP.
   —AND FRIENDS—

RENKA & 2ND GROUP.
   —AND FRIENDS—

ALL.
   —FOR EV'RYONE DEPENDS ON THEIR FRIENDS TILL THE VERY END.

ALL *(or solo CHILD)*.
   WE'LL STICK TOGETHER. AMEN!

IRENA. Very well, everyone. You go along now with Renka. You'll get cleaned up at the bathhouse, then on to supper.

RENKA. Come, come. Quickly now.

Act I I NEVER SAW ANOTHER BUTTERFLY

(The CHILDREN, now in better spirits, exit with RENKA, chattering among themselves. IRENA sees a piece of crumpled paper and picks it up. She begins to straighten it.)

IRENA. Hmm. A duty roster. That will add nicely to my supplies.

(She tucks the paper inside the sheaf, then becomes aware of someone in the shadows. It is RAJA who has entered. She appears younger than before, as she always will when not narrating. She wears a scarf and carries a cloth sack of meager possessions.)

My dear, I didn't see you there.

(Slowly and tensely, RAJA takes a step or two into the light.)

You must run along with the others to the bathhouse now.

(RAJA remains tense, staring straight ahead. A distant siren is heard. She trembles slightly and clutches her bag to herself.)

RAJA. I—I want to be with my mother and father and brother. But the soldiers brought me here.
IRENA *(gently)*. That's because children and adults must go to separate barracks. Come now to the bathhouse where we will clean up for supper.

RAJA *(stepping backward)*. There are stories of people who do not come back from the bathhouses. My friend Irsa told me—

IRENA. That may be true in some places—like Auschwitz—but not here. This is a real bathhouse. You'll be with friends... What is your name? *(RAJA shakes her head and pulls away.)* I am Irena Synkova. I'm a teacher here in Terezin. You'll come to school with us, won't you? *(RAJA turns and drops to the ground, covering her face with her hands. IRENA kneels at a distance from her, talking very quietly.)* You are from Prague? I once taught in Prague. When I first came to Prague, I was about your age. I remember how frightened I was. But after I made some friends, I was happy to live there. Now you are not alone, and you must not be afraid either. *(She reaches for her gently. RAJA allows IRENA to remove her scarf and to take the sack from her clenched fist. She watches IRENA's face.)* Now that you know my name, you must tell me yours. How can we be friends? I won't know what to call you.

RAJA. My number is tattooed here. *(Still watching her, RAJA stretches out her arm and shows a number tattooed on her arm. IRENA, touched by this, caresses her arm gently and smooths her hair. She begins to look through the sack and finds an identification tag.)*

IRENA *(reading the tag)*. Raja Englanderova. *(RAJA watches silently as IRENA carefully replaces the items in her sack. IRENA rises.)* Come, Raja, Raja Englanderova. Let me tell you about our school. *(RAJA slowly rises.)* We have only recently begun, and there will be a new class starting tomorrow. We have very few books, but we sing songs and paint and draw and even write

Act I   I NEVER SAW ANOTHER BUTTERFLY   25

poems. *(Flipping through the sheaf of paper.)* See, I save all the paper I can find—forms, wrapping paper—and when there's enough, the children paint and draw. In tomorrow's class, I'll be handing out the papers I found today. And you can choose a piece for your very own.

(Slowly, RAJA puts her hand on IRENA's arm.)

RAJA. My...name...is...Raja...

(She wearily leans her head on IRENA's shoulder. IRENA embraces her gently. She slowly picks up RAJA's sack and scarf.)

IRENA. Come. I'll walk you to the bathhouse. *(They cross to the edge of the stage. IRENA exits as RAJA stops and turns to the audience as the narrator again.)*

RAJA. In that first brief encounter, I tried to convince myself that this gentle person was real and not an illusion. In time, I would come to know just how real she was—and how much she would mean to all of us.

(Two SOLDIERS enter. Rifles hang from their shoulders, and they carry clipboards. They address an outdoor assemblage which is unseen.)

1ST SOLDIER. Good day, fellow citizens. We trust you have found your first few weeks here agreeable.
2ND SOLDIER. Because of the expected arrival of more of our Jewish constituents, our leaders have determined that a few new rules are now in effect for the betterment of

all. *(They read from their clipboards, rhythmically over music delivered as recitative.)*

(SONG #3: "THE RULES")

1ST SOLDIER *(speaking in rhythm)*.
>THE WOMEN WILL BE SEPARATED FROM THE MEN.
>YOU WILL BE REUNITED, BUT WE DON'T KNOW WHEN.

2ND SOLDIER.
>YOU'RE NOW FORBIDDEN TO WRITE LETTERS ANYMORE.
>YOU MAY NOT WALK UPON THE PAVEMENT AS BEFORE.

1ST SOLDIER.
>ALL CONTACT WITH THE GENTILES IS PROHIBITED.
>RESPECT TO SERVICEMEN MUST BE EXHIBITED.

2ND SOLDIER.
>SO EV'RY SOLDIER THAT YOU SEE, YOU MUST SALUTE.
>AND THERE'S ONE FINAL RULE WE MUST NOW INSTITUTE—

1ST SOLDIER.
>YOU CANNOT USE TOBACCO,

2ND SOLDIER.
>   COFFEE, WINE OR TEA,

1ST SOLDIER.
>   AND IF YOU BREAK A RULE,

2ND SOLDIER.
>   YOUR SENTENCING WILL BE

1ST SOLDIER.
>   A CANING PUNISHMENT

2ND SOLDIER.
>   OF TEN TO FIFTY BLOWS

1ST SOLDIER.
>   OR MAYBE TIME IN PRISON.

BOTH.
>   HOW LONG? WHO KNOWS?

1ST SOLDIER.
>   WE THANK EACH ONE OF YOU FOR YOUR ATTENTION HERE.

BOTH.
>   WE HOPE WE'VE MADE THESE SIMPLE RULES QUITE CRYSTAL CLEAR.

(Speaking as they salute.)
Heil Hitler! *(They exit.)*

(A moment later, several ADULTS enter and cross.)

28 I NEVER SAW ANOTHER BUTTERFLY   Act I

ADULTS *(overlapping speeches)*. We can't write letters anymore?... Careful, don't walk on the pavement!... No tobacco? My pipe was my only pleasure here... They made me hand over both bottles of wine I brought from home... I don't think I can live without tea... Let's hope you're able to... Let's hope we *all* are.
SOLDIER'S VOICE *(from offstage)*. You there! In that group. Men must separate from women.
1ST ADULT *(calling to offstage)*. But we just now learned the rules.
SOLDIER'S VOICE. And the rules are now in effect. Separate!

(In despair, the MEN exit in one direction, the WOMEN in the other. A moment later RAJA enters.)

RAJA. Almost daily, more rules and prohibitions were announced. And *every day*, new transports arrived. Before long, the gentile population was evacuated, leaving only the Jews—and the officials and soldiers, of course. A town that was originally built for eight thousand would soon have a population of almost sixty thousand... But through it all, Irena and Renka persevered.

(She exits as IRENA and RENKA lead the children into the "schoolroom." IRENA carries the sheaf of papers, and RENKA holds paints, crayons and pencils.)

IRENA. All right, children. Now that we've had our morning exercise and sung not one, but *two* new songs, it's time for us to do some work. *Fun* work, that is. Sit down, please. *(The children sit at makeshift desks of*

Act I   I NEVER SAW ANOTHER BUTTERFLY   29

wooden boxes or on the floor itself. IRENA and RENKA dispense the drawing and writing materials.) Today we draw, we paint, we write.

1ST CHILD. What should we draw?

2ND CHILD. What should we paint?

3RD CHILD. What should we write?

IRENA. Anything at all. Something you feel.

RENKA. Something you've seen.

IRENA. Something you like.

4TH CHILD. How about something we *don't* like?

IRENA. Absolutely.

RENKA. Anything that's on your mind.

5TH CHILD. Hey, my paper is all crinkly.

6TH CHILD. Mine has jagged edges.

7TH CHILD. Mine looks like a triangle.

8TH CHILD. Mine has writing on one side.

IRENA. It's true. Most of these papers aren't perfect—new and unmarked—like you were used to at home. But we're not always going to have exactly what we want—or even need. I know *I* didn't.

(SONG #4: "DO THE BEST WITH WHAT YOU'VE GOT")

IRENA *(singing)*.
 WHEN I WAS YOUNG, A LOT LIKE YOU,
 THE THINGS I HAD WERE VERY FEW.
 BUT IF I STARTED TO COMPLAIN,
 MY MOTHER CALMLY WOULD EXPLAIN,
 "WHETHER YOU HAVE A LOT OR NOT,
 ALWAYS DO THE BEST WITH WHAT YOU'VE GOT.

> START WITH YOUR IMAGINATION,
> MIX IT WITH SOME INSPIRATION.
> ADD A DAB OF PERSPIRATION.
> YOU'LL ACCOMPLISH QUITE A LOT.
> JUST DO THE BEST WITH WHAT YOU'VE GOT."

(Speaking.)
Here, I'll give you an example.
(Singing.)
> REMEMBER THE TALE OF THE TORTOISE AND THE HARE?

CHILDREN *(speaking in rhythm)*.
> TORTOISE AND THE HARE?

IRENA.
> THEY ONCE HAD A RACE FROM HERE TO THERE.

CHILDREN *(speaking in rhythm)*.
> HERE TO THERE?

IRENA.
> THE TORTOISE STARTED SLOWLY WHICH MADE THE HARE LAUGH.

(The HARE laughs.)
> SOON THE HARE WAS LEADING BY A MILE-AND-A-HALF.

HARE *(speaking)*. Left him in the dust!

IRENA *(singing)*.
> HE WAS SO FAR AHEAD, THAT COCKY OLD CHAP,

Act I   I NEVER SAW ANOTHER BUTTERFLY   31

> **HE DECIDED TO STOP AND TAKE A LITTLE NAP.**
>
> *(The HARE yawns and lies down.)*
>
> **BUT THE TORTOISE KEPT GOING AND NEVER GAVE IN,**
> **AND BEFORE VERY LONG HE STARTED TO WIN.**

CHILDREN *(or TORTOISE)*.
> **HE (I) STARTED TO WIN.**

IRENA.
> **THEN FIN'LY AT LAST WHEN THE HARE DID AWAKE,**
> **HE KNEW IN AN INSTANT HE HAD MADE A MISTAKE.**

(The HARE wakes up and sees the TORTOISE far ahead.)

HARE *(speaking)*. Now I'm the one left in the dust!

IRENA *(singing)*.
> **HE THEN HUNG HIS HEAD AND STOOD IN DISGRACE,**
> **FOR THE SLOW, STEADY TORTOISE HAD WON THE BIG RACE.**

HARE *(speaking)*. How embarrassing. I can't show my face.

TORTOISE *(singing)*.
> WELL, I CAN'T RUN REAL FAST OR EVEN TROT,
> BUT I DID THE BEST WITH WHAT I'VE GOT.

HARE *(or CHILDREN)*.
> HE DID THE BEST WITH WHAT HE'S GOT.

GROUP 1, 2, 3 & 4 *(overlapping in turn)*.
> START WITH YOUR IMAGINATION,
> MIX IT WITH SOME INSPIRATION,
> ADD A DAB OF PERSPIRATION
> YOU'LL ACCOMPLISH QUITE A LOT.

ALL.
> JUST DO THE BEST WITH WHAT YOU'VE GOT!

RENKA *(speaking)*. May I try one?

IRENA. Sure, go ahead.

RENKA *(speaking in rhythm as she chooses two CHILDREN to play the parts)*.
> HOW ABOUT THE STORY OF THE PRINCESS AND THE FROG?

CHILDREN *(speaking in rhythm)*.
> PRINCESS AND THE FROG?

RENKA *(singing)*.
> THE PRINCESS WAS PERCHED BY A POND ON A LOG.
> HER NECKLACE FELL OFF, AND IT SANK DOWN BELOW,
> AND THE POOR LITTLE PRINCESS CRIED OUT,

Act I I NEVER SAW ANOTHER BUTTERFLY 33

PRINCESS *(speaking in rhythm)*.
OH, NO!

RENKA.
**BUT UP FROM THE WATER A BIG FROG AROSE
WITH THE PRINCESS' NECKLACE RIGHT
THERE ON HIS NOSE.**

PRINCESS.
**OH, THANK YOU! IN WHAT WAY CAN I REPAY
YOU?**

FROG *(speaking in rhythm)*.
IF YOU INSIST, A KISS WILL DO.

RENKA.
SHE KISSED THE FROG WITHOUT A WINCE,

CHILDREN *(speaking in rhythm)*.
WITHOUT A WINCE?

RENKA.
**AND HE SUDDENLY BECAME A HANDSOME
PRINCE.**

PRINCE.
**OH, *MERCI BEAUCOUP*, MY FAIR
MADEMOISELLE.
YOU'VE BROKEN AN AGE-OLD WITCH'S SPELL.
YOU'VE RESCUED A FROG FROM A TERRIBLE
SPOT.**

PRINCESS.
>   **WELL, I DID THE BEST WITH WHAT I'VE GOT.**

(She mimes a kiss in the air, then they hold hands.)

ALL *(except the PRINCE and PRINCESS)*.
>   **SHE DID THE BEST WITH WHAT SHE'S GOT.**

IRENA.
>   **SO, DON'T FORGET MY MOTHER'S SAGE ADVICE.**
>   **HER WISE, WISE WORDS WILL SURELY SUFFICE.**
>   **IF YOU HEED THEM WELL,**
>   **THEN YOU CAN EXCEL—**

IRENA & RENKA.
>   **—BY USING WHAT'S INSIDE OF YOU**
>   **TO ACHIEVE THE THINGS YOU WANT TO DO.**

IRENA.
>   **START WITH YOUR IMAGINATION.**
>   **START WITH YOUR IMAGINATION.**
>   **START WITH YOUR IMAGINATION.**
>   **START WITH YOUR IMAGINATION.**

RENKA *(overlapping IRENA)*.
>   **MIX IT WITH SOME INSPIRATION.**
>   **MIX IT WITH SOME INSPIRATION.**
>   **MIX IT WITH SOME INSPIRATION.**

Act I   I NEVER SAW ANOTHER BUTTERFLY   35

CHILDREN GROUP 1 *(overlapping IRENA and RENKA)*.
ADD A DAB OF PERSPIRATION.
ADD A DAB OF PERSPIRATION.

CHILDREN GROUP TWO *(overlapping)*.
YOU'LL ACCOMPLISH QUITE A LOT—

ALL.
JUST DO THE BEST WITH WHAT YOU'VE GOT.

IRENA.
JUST DO THE VERY—

CHILD SOLO ONE.
VERY—

CHILD SOLO TWO.
VERY—

ALL.
BEST WITH WHAT YOU'VE GOT!

5TH CHILD. You know, the crinkles in my paper look like waves. I think I'll paint a picture of the ocean on it.
6TH CHILD. These jagged edges on *my* paper remind me of the pine tree in our backyard. I think I'll write a poem about a tree.
7TH CHILD. My triangle looks like a sailing ship.
5TH CHILD. We can glue your ship onto my ocean.

(The 7TH CHILD enthusiastically joins the 5TH CHILD, and they begin to work.)

8TH CHILD. I know what I can do with this paper that has writing on one side.

IRENA. What's that, dear?

8TH CHILD. I'll write on the *other* side.

IRENA. Very good.

RENKA. All right. Everybody to work. I'll be here to help if you need me.

1ST CHILD. May I have a red crayon, please?

RENKA. Yes, I think I have one here.

(She goes to the 1ST CHILD and gives her the crayon. Silently, she proceeds to the others, helping them. The younger RAJA tentatively enters and stands at the edge of the classroom until IRENA notices her.)

IRENA *(going to RAJA)*. Raja. You decided to come. Good. Would you like to join the others? *(RAJA slowly nods her head.)* Very well then. You may sit right here. I'll bring you some paper and a pencil and paints. *(RAJA slowly sits as IRENA gathers some materials and brings them to RAJA.)* Write or draw anything you wish.

(RAJA slowly, laboriously begins to write as IRENA goes back to the CHILDREN. She and RENKA quietly observe their works. After a moment, RAJA stands and looks at what she has written.)

RAJA. Slowly, I began to heal. It was months before I could say anything but, "My name is Raja." At first, all I wrote was my name in stiff, crippled letters: Raja! Raja! Raja! It helped me to be sure I was still alive, that

Act I I NEVER SAW ANOTHER BUTTERFLY 37

I still knew my name—Raja... Then one day I wrote another name.

(She writes, then holds the paper out to IRENA who crosses to her and takes it.)

IRENA *(reading)*. "Irena." You wrote my name—Irena.

(They embrace. IRENA takes the materials from her and returns to the children. She, RENKA and the children begin to exit.)

RAJA. Then I knew I was healed. I could paint and draw and speak again. I could tell Irena the things I was remembering. The life I had left began to come back to me.

(The voice of Raja's MOTHER is heard.)

MOTHER *(from offstage)*. Raja!
RAJA. I was no longer afraid to remember.
MOTHER. Raja!
RAJA. Yes, Mother.
MOTHER *(still from offstage as all except RAJA exit)*. Cover the bread—and close the door to the kitchen. The candles will go out.

(She enters with candles and readies a table for the Sabbath. RAJA takes a few steps toward offstage and mimes looking through a window.)

RAJA *(entering the scene from the darkness)*. Papa's coming up the street. I can see him from the window.

MOTHER *(sharply)*. Raja, you must not open the shutters. I've told you that...do you hear?

(PAVEL enters as RAJA mimes closing the shutters.)

PAVEL. She'll get us all in trouble!

MOTHER. She'll be careful. *(Calling.)* Come, it's time to light the Sabbath.

RAJA. Without Papa? He's coming...

MOTHER. Then he will be here. Come away from the window now.

(MOTHER turns, relieved, as FATHER enters.)

MOTHER. Papa, at last!

FATHER *(with false ease)*. All right, Mama, all right. I'm late, but...

RAJA *(running to him)*. I saw you from the window, so you weren't really late, Papa.

FATHER *(kissing her)*. Of course not—as long as I am in sight, I'm not late.

(He removes his coat, stepping into the center with an affectionate but tired embrace for MOTHER. She begins to light the candles, and suddenly the room is filled with the sounds of low-flying planes. They are dangerously close and the family cringes, following the sound of each plane as it flies over the roof. PAVEL runs to the window to look. MOTHER quickly draws him back.)

Act I   I NEVER SAW ANOTHER BUTTERFLY   39

MOTHER. Pavel! Come away from the window. We must keep the shutters closed...you know that.

PAVEL. Nazis. So close you can see the damned swastikas on the wings.

MOTHER. Pavel! The Sabbath!

PAVEL. Sabbath Eve—and the Nazis about to join us.

RAJA *(attentive)*. They're gone now...

FATHER *(intently, to his son)*. Be careful—we must all be careful. Tonight the planes, tomorrow...

MOTHER. Tomorrow? Josef, what do you mean?

FATHER. Mama, Pavel, Raja... *(Almost in tears.)* Today—today, I lost my job.

MOTHER. Josef, it can't be true...

FATHER. We all knew it had to come.

MOTHER. But you were promised.

FATHER. Promises! What do they mean? I must report to work at Litomerice—they are building a station...

RAJA. But, Papa, you're not a carpenter. You're a teacher.

FATHER. I must learn manual labor. Imagine—all of us at the school—all of us. We were given one hour to clear away—books, papers, everything. One hour after all those years.

MOTHER. What next?

FATHER. We will have to move—again... *(Helplessly.)* The landlord is German—and we are—

PAVEL *(angrily)*. Jews!

FATHER. We...are...Jews... And we must all of us move into the area of the old ghetto.

MOTHER. How soon?

FATHER. Tomorrow. By sundown.

PAVEL. They give us the Sabbath to move?

MOTHER *(trying to understand the whole impact of the orders)*. Wait. You said everybody at the school. What about Vera?

FATHER. Yes. Your sister, too. All the women were released to work in the streets. Married *and* unmarried.

PAVEL *(realizing the import of this)*. Irca!

FATHER. Irca, as well.

PAVEL. Where is she?

FATHER. They were turned out in the streets—with the rest.

PAVEL. But we thought the Jewish council was going to appeal?

FATHER. There have been…meetings.

PAVEL. Talk!

FATHER. Talk is better than what you do. *(He is beginning to show his anger.)* Shout slogans, you—and your friends— *(derisively)* —be brave!

PAVEL. Better than hiding behind your prayer shawls!

(FATHER rises, affronted, and stands staring at PAVEL.)

MOTHER. Pavel, you go too far.

PAVEL. At least shouting lets the Nazis know we're alive.

FATHER. You go too far…too far… *(He is limp from controlling his anger. He sits wearily and then turns to speak directly to PAVEL.)* You think we don't know—last night, your joke, at the Regional Theatre? Pavel, you know Jews are not allowed to…

PAVEL. A little joke on the guards. *(With uneasy bravado.)* So we stoned the lights in the street and attacked them from ambush. They never knew what happened to them.

FATHER. A joke! Not so amusing this morning. Hanus was taken, his number called before the rest. He is on the train now.

PAVEL. Why Hanus? He wasn't even there.

FATHER. A Nazi guard said he recognized him among the "pranksters."

PAVEL. And the council didn't intervene? No one protested? What cowards.

FATHER *(with hurt anger)*. Pavel!

PAVEL. No wonder our star is yellow!

FATHER *(striking him across the mouth)*. You go too far...too far. *(He turns, ashamed.)*

PAVEL *(ashamed, but angry)*. Papa, I'm...sorry, but...

FATHER. But you do not understand...you cannot.

PAVEL. I understand. I have this to remind me! *(Gestures to the star on his jacket.)*

MOTHER *(finally losing her composure)*. What is this talk? The star cannot destroy us—but I will tell you what can... *(She turns on the boy roughly.)* Losing the necessities of life—food, shelter, our schools, our synagogues.

PAVEL. I know, Mama. But—

MOTHER *(reaching a point of exhaustion)*. It means for all of us separation—and the fear of separation—planes today, tanks tomorrow and always, the guards, the Nazis. You and your foolish bravado!... *(Breaking down with her own weariness and fear.)* And we may all be lost...all—lost.

PAVEL. I know, Mama. I see what's going on, but to just endure. It seems so...

FATHER. Weak? To you, it's weak. But think—the Nazis want us to work for them. If we must work, we must eat. There's that chance for life.

PAVEL. I don't call this living!

MOTHER *(recovering)*. But while we live, we stay together, and perhaps later...

FATHER. Yes...if they bid us work, then we will eat, and we may survive—together—this war. It cannot last much longer...

PAVEL *(giving in to his father's optimism)*. All right, Papa.

FATHER. All right, all right. So, no more shouting and no more jokes on Nazi guards. In a few months we'll be back in our flat. The landlord has promised to keep the furniture for us—he does not wish us harm. It will be here when we come back.

PAVEL *(wearily)*. Yes, Papa.

FATHER. And you and Irca will be married, as we planned, you will see...I promise...

PAVEL *(laughing wryly)*. Promises.

FATHER. You will see. *(Cheerfully.)* Come now, Mama, light the candles.

(MOTHER assumes her place at the table and begins to light the Sabbath candles. As she does, lights dim. Searchlights flash through the windows and light up the faces of the group. They become tense, but MOTHER and FATHER continue with the ceremony.)

Act I   I NEVER SAW ANOTHER BUTTERFLY   43

(SONG #5: "WELCOME SHABBAT")

MOTHER *(singing)*.
>AS THE SUN GOES DOWN,
>LET US GATHER 'ROUND
>AND WELCOME SHABBAT.

FATHER.
>ON THIS SACRED DAY
>WE WILL GLADLY PRAY
>AND WELCOME SHABBAT.

MOTHER & FATHER.	RAJA & PAVEL.
ANGELS OF PEACE DESCEND, HOLY AND BLESSED. AND NOW THE SETTING SUN BIDS US TO REST	**OOO...**
	PAVEL.
RAJA.	**AHH...**
AS THE CANDLES GLOW WE SING THE SONGS WE KNOW TO WELCOME SHABBAT.	

PAVEL.
>WHEN THE SABBATH BRIDE
>IS WITH US BY OUR SIDE
>WE WELCOME SHABBAT.

RAJA & PAVEL.　　　　　　　　　MOTHER & FATHER.
 STARS FILL A DARK'NING
 SKY
 WITH A GENTLE LIGHT.　　**OOO...**
 AS YOU WATCH OVER US,
 DAY TURNS TO NIGHT.

            FATHER.
            AHH...

ALL.
 COME OH SABBATH QUEEN,
 SO LOVELY AND SERENE,
 WE WELCOME SHABBAT.
 WITH YOUR LOVE AROUND US,
 JOY AND PEACE HAVE FOUND US.

ALL *(except MOTHER)*.
 WELCOME SHABBAT.

MOTHER.　　　　　　　　　　　　RAJA & PAVEL.
 WELCOME SHABBAT.　　　**OOO...**
 WELCOME SHABBAT.

FATHER.
 WELCOME SHABBAT.
 WELCOME SHABBAT.

(MOTHER extinguishes the candles as ALL except RAJA exit.)

RAJA. Yes, the memories began to come back to me. Even unpleasant memories are better than no memories at all... We moved in with Irca's family. And then we had

Act I I NEVER SAW ANOTHER BUTTERFLY

to move again. Finally, the day came when it was our turn to board the transport.

(A shrill train whistle is heard as the TWO SOLDIERS enter.)

1ST SOLDIER *(to an unseen group)*. Jews—*Achtung!* Step quickly!
2ND SOLDIER. Men left! Women and children right!
1ST SOLDIER. Keep moving!
BOTH. *Schnell! Schnell!*

(They exit. Offstage voices are heard, perhaps accompanied by the sound of a moving train. RAJA looks into the distance, remembering.)

1ST VOICE *(child)*. Where's Father? What happened to Father?
2ND VOICE *(woman)*. You'll see him at the camp. Quiet now.
3RD VOICE *(child)*. I'm thirsty.
4TH VOICE *(child)*. I'm hungry.
5TH VOICE *(woman)*. Wait…just a little while, and we'll have food.
6TH VOICE *(child)*. When will we be there? Will Father be there?
7TH VOICE *(woman)*. Patience.
8TH VOICE *(child)*. Where are we going now? What are they doing in that room there?
9TH VOICE *(woman)*. We'll see. We must wait our turn.
10TH VOICE *(child)*. They told me to remember the number tattooed on my arm.

11TH VOICE *(woman)*. Yes. At roll call they will ask your number.

12TH VOICE *(child)*. They laughed and told us we were marked, like pigs.

13TH VOICE *(child)*. They said—it will never go away.

RAJA. Before long, I, too, was one of them—the children of Terezin. One who saw everything—the barbed-wire fence, the rats, the lice—one who knew hunger, dirt and smells—one who heard trains arrive and leave and the tread of heavy feet in the dark. But we were the luckier ones. After two years, we still had Irena Synkova's classroom in which to write and paint the stories of those days.

(The CHILDREN enter, writing and drawing. They form a semicircle and remain standing. RAJA takes her place at one end of the semicircle. IRENA and RENKA enter. IRENA hands a sheet of paper and pencil to RAJA who begins writing.)

IRENA. Boys and girls, I'm very proud of the work you've been doing. I hope you know that I've been keeping your pictures and poems and stories in a safe place, so that no one can destroy them.

RENKA. Do the very best you can. Who knows who may see your work some day.

(The CHILDREN begin to recite as they write and draw. Underscore 5A begins.)

Act I I NEVER SAW ANOTHER BUTTERFLY

RAJA. I never saw another butterfly...
   The last, the very last,
   So richly, brightly, dazzlingly yellow.
1ST CHILD. I haven't seen my mother in so long. I shall draw her picture, and she will always be with me.
RAJA. Perhaps if the sun's tears sing
   against a white stone...
   Such, such a yellow
   Is carried lightly 'way up high.
2ND CHILD. The buildings now are fuller, body smelling close to body, the garrets scream with light for long, long hours.
RAJA. It went away I'm sure because it wished to kiss the world goodbye.
3RD CHILD. In Terezin in the so-called park
   A queer old granddad sits.
   He wears a beard down to his lap
   And on his head a little cap.
RAJA. Though it is gone,
   Other colorful things remain behind.
4TH CHILD. Another day has gone for keeps
   Into the bottomless pit of time.
   Dawn crawls along the ghetto streets
   Embracing all who walk this way.
RAJA. The dandelions call to me,
   And the white chestnut candles in the court.
5TH CHILD. I caught six fleas and three bedbugs today. I have drawn them carefully to remember my fine hunt.
RAJA. Only I never saw another butterfly.
6TH CHILD. Last night I had a beautiful dream. I was home; I saw our flat and our street.
RAJA. That butterfly was the last one.

7TH CHILD. My friend left today. I saw her in one of the cars as the train was pulling away.

RAJA. Butterflies don't live here in the ghetto.

8TH CHILD. I said goodbye to my bunkmate this morning. He (she) reports to the transport at noon.

RAJA. I never saw another butterfly.

(Each, in turn—RAJA first—hands his/her work to IRENA and RENKA respectively and exits. IRENA and RENKA then exit. A moment later, a train is heard pulling away from the station. HONZA, a boy of sixteen, enters running.)

HONZA. No—no! Not Jiri. *(Calling and waving to the unseen departing train.)* Jiri! Jiri! *(He slumps down.)* I didn't even have a chance to say goodbye.

(RAJA enters, watching after the now departed train. She and HONZA are unaware of each other.)

RAJA. Thank God. None of them are on the train today. Once again we live at least till tomorrow.

HONZA. Jiri—they said they wouldn't take him. He was a plumber, an electrician—so clever—they said they wouldn't take him...

RAJA *(noticing HONZA, crossing and kneeling beside him)*. Everyone goes—eventually... Jiri? Was he your friend?

HONZA. He was my brother.

RAJA. Wait...I think he was a friend of *my* brother. My name is Raja. My brother is Pavel.

HONZA. Yes. He's spoken of *you*. And Irca.

Act I I NEVER SAW ANOTHER BUTTERFLY 49

RAJA *(glancing about quietly)*. They wish to be married while they're here.

HONZA. I know. But what's the good of that?

RAJA. At least they'll be together.

HONZA. Only if they can break away from their separate barracks long enough for a secret ceremony.

RAJA. Even so—married, they'll be together spiritually.

HONZA. And what's the good of that?

RAJA. Together they will not be afraid. That's the good. *(A pause.)*

HONZA. Are you afraid?

RAJA. What if I am?... Do you think I'm a coward?

HONZA *(a slight laugh)*. I think—you don't know if you are or not.

RAJA. Why are you laughing at me?

HONZA. I am laughing at you because—you are a girl.

RAJA. I'm glad you noticed.

(SONG #6: "YOU DON'T KNOW...")

HONZA *(singing)*.
> **YOU ARE A GIRL, AND YOU DON'T KNOW THE FIRST THING ABOUT ANYTHING.**

RAJA.
> **I AM A GIRL, AND I KNOW THE FIRST THING ABOUT MANY THINGS.**

HONZA *(speaking)*. Like what? Go ahead and say.

RAJA *(singing)*
> LIKE THE FIRST LETTER OF THE ALPHABET IS "A."

HONZA.
> OKAY...THAT'S ONE.

RAJA.
> I'VE JUST BEGUN.
> WHEN I'M COUNTING, THE FIRST NUMBER I COME TO—IS ONE.

HONZA.
> IT'S TRUE. THAT'S TWO.

RAJA.
> AND I'M NOT THROUGH.
> I BELIEVE THE FIRST PEOPLE ON EARTH WERE ADAM AND EVE.

HONZA.
> THAT'S THREE. PERHAPS YOU ARE NOT SO NAIVE AFTER ALL.

RAJA.
> SEPTEMBER TWENTY-ONE IS THE FIRST DAY OF FALL.
> MERCURY'S THE FIRST PLANET FROM THE SUN.
> LAUGHTER IS THE FIRST SIGN YOU'RE HAVING FUN.

Act I I NEVER SAW ANOTHER BUTTERFLY 51

HONZA.
>IT SEEMS I MAY HAVE MISJUDGED YOU.

RAJA.
>IF YOU DON'T MIND, I'M STILL NOT THROUGH.
>BEFORE A GIRL MARRIES, SHE FIRST IS A MISS.
>AND WHEN SHE'S IN LOVE, SHE GETS HER FIRST KISS.

HONZA.
>IT'S CLEAR YOU KNOW SEV'RAL FIRST THINGS,
>SO WHY DON'T WE STOP OUR BICKERINGS?

RAJA.
>YOU STARTED IT, IF YOU RECALL,
>BY ACTING LIKE A KNOW-IT-ALL.
>ANYWAY, I HAVE ONE MORE FIRST TO CLAIM.
>I EVEN KNOW YOUR FIRST NAME.

HONZA *(speaking)*. You know my first name?
RAJA. And your last one, too. The first name is Honza. The last is Kozek.

(He reacts in surprise.)

HONZA *(singing)*.
>YOU ARE CORRECT, I MUST ADMIT.
>I HAVE SHORTCHANGED YOU BY QUITE A BIT.
>I SUBMIT YOU'VE CLIPPED MY WINGS,
>FOR YOU DO KNOW THE FIRST THING ABOUT MANY THINGS.

BOTH.
>   **YES, I (YOU) DO KNOW THE FIRST THING
>   ABOUT MANY THINGS.**

HONZA.
>   **AND IF YOU PLEASE, I'M DOWN ON MY KNEES**
>   *(He kneels.)*
>   **TO OFFER MY APOLOGIES.**

RAJA *(pulling HONZA up).*
>   **WHEN ONE ADMITS THAT HE IS WRONG,
>   IT SHOWS THAT HE IS VERY STRONG.
>   THEREFORE, I ACCEPT YOUR APOLOGY
>   AND WHAT SEEMS TO BE YOUR SINCERITY—
>   WHEN YOU SAY—**

HONZA.
>   **THAT YOU DO—**

RAJA.
>   **IT IS TRUE—**

HONZA.
>   **—KNOW THE VERY FIRST THING—**

RAJA.
>   **—KNOW THE—**

BOTH.
>   **—VERY FIRST THING ABOUT MANY THINGS.
>   YES, I (YOU) KNOW.**

Act I   I NEVER SAW ANOTHER BUTTERFLY   53

(They shake hands, draw closer, hold for a moment, then back off.)

HONZA. I think—you are not a coward after all.

RAJA. And *I* think—neither are you.

HONZA. Maybe. *(A pause.)* My father was beaten and left for dead before my eyes. I saw it. I couldn't move, I was so afraid. But I didn't run. I never understood it—until my father, dying, told me, "You're a good boy, Honza: you are afraid, but you are not a coward."

RAJA *(touching his shoulder)*. I'm sorry... *(Reluctantly.)* I must go. We really shouldn't be seen together.

HONZA. The guards don't usually hang around after the trains leave... Where do you live?

RAJA. Number twenty-five. And you?

HONZA. House number two—on the other side, near the wall.

RAJA *(eager to talk)*. There are thirty girls—in our group—most of us from Prague...Irena...she's in charge of the whole compound—she lives with us.

HONZA. We live alone. We elect our own leader—and we have meetings—secret ones. We also work in the fields.

RAJA. So do we—some of us. I do. I'm old enough.

HONZA. I'm our leader now. I was elected.

RAJA *(impressed)*. Oh. What does a leader do?

HONZA. Make plans. Meet with the leaders from other boys' homes. We're working on something right now.

RAJA. What?

HONZA *(lowering his voice)*. We're going to have a newspaper and report the news in camp.

RAJA. Have you got a printing press?

HONZA. We don't need one. We'll make handwritten copies of the news and hang them around in the barracks. It's my idea.

RAJA. Would you put one in the girls' home?

HONZA. I suppose we could— I never thought about it.

RAJA. I'd copy it over—I could do that.

HONZA. I'd have to talk about it with the rest. I suppose it's a good idea... Well, I guess I've got to go now— we're going to have a meeting about the paper. I—I could see you tomorrow—and let you know how it goes.

RAJA. That would be good.

HONZA. I'll meet you behind your barrack—about this time?

RAJA. Yes.

HONZA. Goodbye. *(He exits.)*

(RAJA moves to center.)

RAJA. And so, the newspaper, *Vedem*, was born, and it helped *us* feel *re*born. We eagerly awaited each copy that was posted in the barracks. The paper was a line of communication that helped the youth of Terezin grow up together... Even though I was only a little older than most of the students in Irene's classroom, I began to feel much older. Honza and I met whenever we could. We would talk...discuss the newspaper. He was headstrong, and sometimes that would annoy me. But when we were apart, I would miss him. *(She exits.)*

(The CHILDREN, except RAJA, enter carrying work materials. They sit at desks—or on the floor—and begin to write, draw or paint half-heartedly.)

Act I   I NEVER SAW ANOTHER BUTTERFLY   55

1ST CHILD. Where's Raja today?
2ND CHILD. Probably with her boyfriend.
3RD CHILD. He's not a boyfriend.
2ND CHILD. How do you know?
3RD CHILD. That's what she told me. She just helps him with the newspaper—*Vedem.*
4TH CHILD. She also takes our writing and artwork to him to hide.
5TH CHILD. Shh. Nobody's supposed to know that.
4TH CHILD. There's no one here but us.
6TH CHILD. Remember what Renka said—the walls have ears.

(IRENA enters carrying some papers.)

IRENA. Hello again. Were you busy working while I was out collecting papers?... Isn't it wonderful that the people in other barracks are helping us find materials to work with. *(She looks over their shoulders at the largely unfilled pages.)* My, my. It looks as though maybe we've been doing more talking than writing and painting this morning.
7TH CHILD. It's finally warming up. I'd rather go outside.
8TH CHILD. We have new assigned times to be outdoors. You know that.
1ST CHILD. More rules.
2ND CHILD. I couldn't think of anything to draw.
3RD CHILD. Or write.
4TH CHILD. Me either.
5TH CHILD. Me either.
IRENA. Well, let's *see*. I know that each of you has a good imagination. *And* a dab of perspiration— *(mopping her*

brow) —especially on a warm day like this. *(The CHILDREN laugh.)* So all we're lacking is—what?
CHILDREN. Inspiration.
IRENA. Exactly. So let's see if I can help in that area. Where would all of you like to be more than anywhere else in the world right now?
6TH CHILD *(holding up his/her hand)*. I know.
IRENA. Yes?
6TH CHILD. Back home.
7TH CHILD. Yes. Back home in Prague.
8TH CHILD. Me, too. *(The other CHILDREN verbally agree.)*
IRENA. That's what I thought.

(RENKA enters.)

RENKA. Irena, the residents of barrack seventeen have collected two large boxes of papers and even a few pencils and crayons.
IRENA. Excellent. I'll go and help you bring them down… So, children, while Renka and I are gone, write or draw or paint what you would most want to do when you go back home. *(She and RENKA exit as the CHILDREN enthusiastically begin to work.)*

(SONG #7: " WHEN I GO HOME")

1ST CHILD *(singing)*.
**WHEN I GO HOME, I'LL BAKE A BIG CAKE
AND EAT SO MUCH MY TUMMY WILL ACHE.**

Act I I NEVER SAW ANOTHER BUTTERFLY   57

2ND CHILD.
> **WHEN I GO HOME, AT LAST I WILL SEE**
> **MY DOLLS WHO'VE ALL BEEN WAITING FOR**
> **ME.**

1ST CHILD.
> **WHEN I GO HOME.**

2ND CHILD.
> **WHEN I GO HOME.**

1ST CHILD.
> **WHEN I GO HOME.**

2ND CHILD.
> **WHEN I GO HOME.**

1ST CHILD.
> **WHEN I GO HOME.**

BOTH.
> **WHEN I GO HOME.**

3RD CHILD.
> **WHEN I GO HOME, I'LL PLAY EV'RY DAY**
> **WITH FRIENDS I'VE MISSED WHILE I WAS**
> **AWAY.**

4TH CHILD.
> **WHEN I GO HOME, I'LL RUN TO THE PARK**
> **AND FEED THE PIGEONS UNTIL IT GETS DARK.**
> **WHEN I GO HOME.**

1ST & 2ND CHILDREN.
    WHEN I GO HOME.

3RD & 4TH CHILDREN.
    WHEN I GO HOME.

1ST & 2ND CHILDREN.
    WHEN I GO HOME.

3RD & 4TH CHILDREN.
    WHEN I GO HOME.

1ST, 2ND, 3RD & 4TH CHLDREN.
    WHEN I GO HOME.

5TH CHILD.
    WHEN I GO HOME, I'LL SLEEP TILL IT'S NOON,
    THEN TAKE A BATH UNTIL I'M A PRUNE.

6TH CHILD.
    WHEN I GO HOME, I'LL PLAY MY TROMBONE
    SO LOUD THAT ALL THE NEIGHBORS WILL
        GROAN.

4TH, 5TH & 6TH CHILDREN.
    WHEN I GO HOME.

1ST, 2ND & 3RD CHILDREN
    WHEN I GO HOME.

4TH, 5TH & 6TH CHILDREN.
    WHEN I GO HOME.

Act I   I NEVER SAW ANOTHER BUTTERFLY   59

1ST, 2ND & 3RD CHILDREN.
   WHEN I GO HOME.

4TH, 5TH & 6TH CHILDREN.
   WHEN I GO HOME.

1ST, 2ND, 3RD, 4TH, 5TH & 6TH CHILDREN.
   WHEN I GO HOME.

7TH CHILD.
   **WHEN I GO HOME, I'LL SAY A SHORT PRAYER,
   AND THANK MY GOD I'M FIN'LY THERE.**

(All smile and murmur in agreement.)

8TH CHILD.
   **WHEN I GO HOME, THE FIRST THING I'LL DO
   IS HOPE YOU'RE SAFE, YOUR FAMILY, TOO.**

(All smile.)

5TH, 6TH, 7TH & 8TH CHILDREN.
   WHEN I GO HOME.

1ST, 2ND, 3RD & 4TH CHILDREN.
   WHEN I GO HOME.

5TH, 6TH, 7TH & 8TH CHILDREN.
   WHEN I GO HOME.

1ST, 2ND, 3RD & 4TH CHILDREN.
   WHEN I GO HOME.

1ST SOLDIER'S VOICE *(offstage, speaking)*. *Achtung!*
2ND SOLDIER'S VOICE *(offstage)*. *Achtung!*
1ST SOLDIER'S VOICE. The following numbers are called: 93877 through 94108...

5TH, 6TH, 7TH & 8TH CHILDREN *(singing, a bit shaken)*.
WHEN I GO HOME.

2ND SOLDIER'S VOICE *(speaking)*. 96724 through 96903. *(The VOICE begins to fade.)* And now the names...

ALL CHILDREN *(or 1ST CHILD, singing)*.
WHEN...I...GO...HOME...

CURTAIN—END OF ACT ONE

ACT TWO

(The two SOLDIERS enter.)

(SONG #8: "CURFEW")

1ST SOLDIER *(singing)*.
CURFEW! OFF THE SIDEWALKS!

2ND SOLDIER.
CURFEW! OFF THE SIDEWALKS!

BOTH.
**CURFEW! OFF THE SIDEWALKS!
CURFEW! OFF THE SIDEWALKS!**

1ST SOLDIER *(to an unseen group)*. To your barracks. Now!

2ND SOLDIER. All residents of barracks eight, thirteen and twenty-nine—you are hereby confined to quarters due to the typhoid outbreak!

1ST SOLDIER. You there—no talking! Go to your barrack, or you will be caned! Ten blows! *(Speaking in rhythm.)*
CURFEW! OFF THE SIDEWALKS!
(After a pause, speaking to 2ND SOLDIER.) They do not move quickly enough.

2ND SOLDIER. Perhaps they do not have the energy. Would you, if your only meal of the day was a bowl of salty soup and two or three potatoes?

1ST SOLDIER. I would do as I was ordered.

2ND SOLDIER. But it would be easier if you dined on meats and cheeses such as we do.

1ST SOLDIER. Which is why we are the guards, and they are the prisoners. Come, Kurt, are you getting soft on these people?

2ND SOLDIER. You have no wife or children, Rolf. I do. I think I would not want them to be treated this way.

1ST SOLDIER. But *your* wife and children are German. These are— *(tossing it off)* —Jews.

2ND SOLDIER. Is there—such a difference?

1ST SOLDIER *(a brief pause, threatening slightly)*. I wonder if the commandant might be interested in hearing that question.

2ND SOLDIER *(quickly)*. I meant nothing by it. Of course, they are—Jews. *(Not convincingly.)* Only Jews.

1ST SOLDIER. Yes... Are you going to play cards at the officers' club tonight?

2ND SOLDIER. I think not. My wife—

1ST SOLDIER *(again with a bit of a threat)*. I advise you to be there, Kurt. The commandant is playing tonight, and we need someone to lose money to him—as usual. I think it may be your turn. *(Turning and calling out.)* You there! Stragglers! To your barracks, or I'll take your numbers, and you'll both pay tomorrow! Ten blows each—or more! *(A pause, then to 2ND SOLDIER.)* See? They can muster the energy when they have to.

2ND SOLDIER. Come. Let's go to the officers' club and get it over with. *(They exit.)*

Act II I NEVER SAW ANOTHER BUTTERFLY   63

(RAJA enters nervously, looking about.)

HONZA'S VOICE *(from offstage)*. Raja?
RAJA. I'm here. *(HONZA enters carrying a copy of* Vedem.*)* Is this week's *Vedem* ready?
HONZA. Here it is...
RAJA *(takes the paper)*. I'll take it and get started. *(She turns.)*
HONZA. Wait...I was thinking... We've talked about it at the meeting... We could run some of the poems from the girls' house—when there's room.
RAJA. Good. Irena will be glad of that. I'll tell her. *(She turns to leave, almost reluctantly.)* I'll see you...
HONZA. Wait...I saw you in the field today. Of course, I couldn't say anything.
RAJA. I know. I saw you—across the road.
HONZA. Maybe we could plan a way to meet there—in case...there are messages...or anything.
RAJA. It wouldn't be safe! The guards are everywhere.
HONZA. We meet here...at night.
RAJA. The guards think we're inside the barracks.
HONZA. I'm not afraid...are you?
RAJA. No...yes, I guess I am. They'd beat you.
HONZA. It wouldn't be the first time. I always get up again.
RAJA. Someday...
HONZA. Someday, maybe, I won't, I suppose. What difference does it make?
RAJA. Don't talk like that. I'll go if you do. *(Starts to leave.)*
HONZA. Wait...wait. I'm only teasing.

RAJA. It would be lonesome without you. I mean, the boys need you—and the paper. Irena says you're the only one she can trust to bury the drawings and the poems.

HONZA. Others could do that.

RAJA. Anyway...*I* would miss you. *(A bit awkwardly.)* Good night. *(She starts to leave, but HONZA takes her arm.)*

HONZA. Raja...wait. I—I have a gift for you. I hid it over here in case the guards came. If they found me with it, I'd be in trouble for sure. *(He exits momentarily, then reenters carrying a small package.)*

RAJA. What is it?

HONZA *(handing her the package)*. Open it carefully. It's very precious.

RAJA *(opening the package)*. I can't imagine— *(Withdrawing a small block of yellow cheese.)* —Cheese!

HONZA *(taking out a small knife and cutting off two slices)*. It had two or three spots of mold on it. I cut them off, and it's as good as new. *(He hands her the slices, and she gives one back to him.)*

RAJA. Cheese. Honza, you're wonderful. I haven't tasted cheese since we've been here. *(They eat the slices.)* Where did you get it?

HONZA. I liberated it.

RAJA. Liberated it? Honza...

HONZA *(cutting off another slice and handing it to her)*. Actually, I took it.

RAJA. You *stole* it. *(She takes a bite out of the slice.)* No wonder it tastes so good. *(She looks at him lovingly as she finishes the slice.)*

Act II   I NEVER SAW ANOTHER BUTTERFLY   65

(SONG #9: "THE GIFT")

RAJA *(singing)*.
>CHEESE...YOU BROUGHT ME CHEESE.
>THERE IS NOTHING THAT I COULD WANT MORE.
>I NEVER THOUGHT I COULD SO ADORE SOMETHING AS PLAIN AS CHEESE.
>BUT, OH, HOW IT PLEASES ME, IT PLEASES ME.
>FOR, YOU SEE, IT IS SOMETHING I WILL NOT ONLY ENJOY,
>BUT IT WAS GIVEN TO ME BY A BOY WHO ALSO PLEASES ME.
>HE WHO GAVE THIS CHEESE TO ME VERY MUCH AGREES WITH ME,
>AND I HOPE HE FEELS THE SAME.

HONZA.
>I WILL NOT WHISPER OR EVEN SPEAK, NO, I WILL EXCLAIM
>THAT I DO FEEL THE SAME ABOUT YOU.

RAJA.
>YOU DO, DO YOU? YOU DO!

HONZA.
>AND I'M SO PLEASED YOU LIKE THE CHEESE.

RAJA.
>I DO.

HONZA.
>YOU ACCEPTED IT WITH SUCH EASE—

RAJA.
    I DID.

HONZA.
    —THAT IT MADE MY SPIRITS SOAR.
    AND WHEN I GET THE CHANCE I'LL BRING
        YOU EVEN MORE.

RAJA.
    CHEESE, YOU BROUGHT ME—

BOTH.
    CHEESE...

RAJA *(kneeling)*.	HONZA.
—AND NOW I'M ON MY KNEES—	CHEESE.
THANKING YOU FOR ALL THAT YOU WENT THROUGH	CHEESE.
TO BRING THIS CHEESE TO ME,	CHEESE.
WHICH I ACCEPT MOST GRATEFULLY	CHEESE. CHEESE.

(HONZA gently lifts her up.)

IT'S BETTER THAN MEATS OR SWEETS—	CHEESE.
TOMATOES, POTATOES—	THAT CHEESE.
THAT CHEESE. THAT	THAT CHEESE.
CHEESE, CAME FROM YOU.	THAT CHEESE.

Act II I NEVER SAW ANOTHER BUTTERFLY   67

>   **AND I PROMISE THAT SOMEHOW,**
>   **WHEN THESE DREARY DAYS ARE THROUGH,**
>   **I, TOO, WILL BRING A CHEESE TO YOU.**

HONZA.
>   **CHEESE!**

RAJA.
>   **CHEESE!**

BOTH.
>   **CHEESE!**

HONZA Wrap it up, and save it for later.
RAJA *(wrapping the cheese)*. Yes. And I will share it with Irena and Renka.
HONZA. Good.
RAJA. I really must go now.
HONZA. I know...I won't be seeing you for a few days.
RAJA. Why?
HONZA. I won't be here.
RAJA *(frightened)*. Honza, what is it?
HONZA. Nothing. A special detail to build something outside the fortifications. They're picking the strongest—I'll be chosen.
RAJA. But—what if something happens?
HONZA. There'll be a chance for extra food. *(Smiles.)* Maybe another cheese.
RAJA. I don't care about the cheese...Honza, I'm afraid!
HONZA. Don't worry... They want the job done—it's some kind of walled courtyard...nothing much can happen... Well, I have to go.

RAJA *(reluctantly)*. Goodbye then... *(HONZA walks into the darkness.)* Goodbye. I'll be waiting...waiting... Please come back. *(She slowly turns to the audience.)* Honza had become very dear to me. And I cherished the feeling. But it also added another feeling—the fear of losing him. *(A pause.)* Fear—this is half the story of Terezin—its beginning, but not its end. I was a child there. I knew that word. I became a woman there, because I learned another word from Irca and Pavel, from Mother and Father, from Irena Synkova. I learned the word "courage" and found the determination to live—to believe in life...even though life all around us was very fragile. Pavel was the first of our family to receive a number for transport away from Terezin. We knew it meant we would never see him again. *(She watches the following scene from a distance.)*

(PAVEL enters carrying a small bag.)

IRCA'S VOICE *(from offstage)*. Pavel! Pavel! *(IRCA enters and runs to PAVEL, taking his hand.)* Pavel, I am coming with you. I settled everything myself, and I have a number in your transport.
PAVEL. Irca, your mother and father need you. Go back to the barracks.
IRCA. Pavel, you are closer to me than parents. I must come with you!

(PAVEL, taking her hand, walks toward the edge of a circle of light and calls quietly.)

PAVEL. Rabbi, we want... Could you marry us, Rabbi?

Act II   I NEVER SAW ANOTHER BUTTERFLY

(The RABBI appears at the edge of the lighted area.)

RABBI. I can. Have you…a wedding ring?
PAVEL. Yes.
RABBI. How much time?
PAVEL. An hour at most.
RABBI. That will be enough. Tell me your Hebrew names…and we must call your parents and some friends.

(Slowly, a few PEOPLE, including PAVEL's parents, enter. A ritual canopy is brought in and held over the young couple. With as much of the ritual as possible, simple and touching, in a makeshift way, a traditional Jewish wedding is performed. The group surrounds the couple as the RABBI addresses them.)

RABBI. Dearly Beloved, in the Torah we read three words, the meaning of which we have never understood as well as today. They are: *Lekh, red, vealita*—go, lower yourself, and you will rise. We, too, have sunk very low but risen very high, because we did not let our sad fate overwhelm us. We have not lost hope that right will finally be victorious over injustice, friendship over hostility, love over hatred, peace over war. May good always arise out of evil.

(SONG #10: "WEDDING PSALM")

RABBI *(blessing PAVEL and IRCA as he sings)*.
**HAPPY ARE THOSE WHO LIVE IN YOUR
HOUSE AND PRAISE YOU ALL DAY LONG.**

IRCA.
> **HAPPY THE PILGRIMS INSPIRED BY YOU,**
> **WE SING YOUR PRAISE IN SONG.**

PAVEL.
> **AS WE WALK THROUGH THE VALLEY OF SORROW,**
> **WE WILL TURN IT TO SPRINGS.**

PAVEL & IRCA.
> **OH GOD OF JACOB, GOD OUR SHIELD,**
> **HEAR US, AND LET YOUR LOVE SHINE.**

RABBI, PAVEL & IRCA.
> **OH GOD OF JACOB, GOD OUR SHIELD,**
> **LOOK ON US NOW AND BE KIND.**

WEDDING GUESTS *(giving their greetings to PAVEL and IRCA)*.
> **HAPPY ARE THOSE WHO LIVE IN YOUR HOUSE**
> **AND PRAISE YOU ALL DAY LONG.**
> **HAPPY THE PILGRIMS INSPIRED BY YOU,**
> **WE SING YOUR PRAISE IN SONG.**

RABBI, PAVEL & IRCA.
> **AS WE WALK THROUGH THE VALLEY OF SORROW,**

ALL.
> **WE WILL TURN IT TO SPRINGS.**

GROUP 1.
> **OH GOD OF JACOB, GOD OUR SHIELD,**

Act II I NEVER SAW ANOTHER BUTTERFLY 71

>**HEAR US, AND LET YOUR LOVE SHINE.**
>**OH GOD OF JACOB, GOD OUR SHIELD,**
>**LOOK ON US NOW, AND BE KIND.**

GROUP 2 *(simultaneously with GROUP 1).*
>**OH GOD, OH GOD, OH GOD, OH SHINE.**
>**GOD, OH GOD, OH GOD, BE KIND.**

GROUP 3 *(simultaneously with GROUPS 1 and 2).*
>**OH GOD, GOD, GOD, SHINE.**
>**GOD, GOD, GOD, BE KIND.**

PAVEL & IRCA.
>**LOOK ON US NOW AND BE KIND.**

(The RABBI blesses a cup of wine given to him by a GUEST.)

RABBI. Blessed art Thou, O Lord our God, King of the Universe, who has created the fruit of the vine.

(He gives the cup to PAVEL, who drinks. PAVEL then gives it to IRCA. After she drinks she returns the cup to the GUEST. MOTHER takes off her wedding ring and gives it to PAVEL with a quiet gesture of affection. He places the ring on IRCA's forefinger. He repeats after the RABBI:)

PAVEL. Thou art consecrated to me with the ring as my wife, according to the faith of Moses and Israel.

(The wedding couple and the RABBI exchange positions. The RABBI then pronounces the benediction.)

RABBI. May the Lord bless you and protect you. May the Lord show you favor and be gracious to you. May the Lord turn in loving kindness to you and grant you peace. Amen.

(The canopy is removed. FATHER steps forward and presents PAVEL with a glass and a kerchief. He wraps the kerchief around the glass, places it on the floor and steps on it. "The breaking of the glass" is intended to temper the joy of the occasion by reminding those present of the destruction of the Temple in Jerusalem and of other calamities that befell the Jewish people. At the moment PAVEL breaks the glass, the sound of an approaching train is heard. ALL except RAJA slowly exit.)

RAJA. One by one the transports came. Mother, Father, Pavel, Irca—they went. Everyone I knew and loved in Prague. There was no one who could remember me before I had come here as a child of twelve...but there were many left standing at the train as the transports started up, the cars crowded, boarded, sealed... *(Sound of a train departing is heard. RAJA follows the sound as it leaves. As her eyes move across the stage she sees HONZA who enters. They embrace.)* Oh, Honza. Thank God you're back—and safe. Life is so contradictory. I lose my family—I regain you. They are all gone, just like *your* family. Now we are both alone.

HONZA. No...we have each other. As long as there is that, we will never be alone.

(IRENA enters.)

Act II I NEVER SAW ANOTHER BUTTERFLY   73

IRENA. Raja, I heard. The last of your family have gone to— resettlement.

RAJA. You can use the word, Irena. Auschwitz. We'll all wind up there—eventually. They've already taken Zdenka and Eve and Mariam and Marianne...

IRENA. I know.

RAJA. Gabriella and Zuzanna...

IRENA. I know...I know...

RAJA. I miss them so much. And I know you do, too. But at least you have lost no family.

IRENA. How do you know?

RAJA. You would have told me, I think. We are close friends.

IRENA. I did not tell you, because you were a child. But I have seen you grow—you and Honza, together. Today, you are no longer children—and so I will tell you. I have a child—she is nine years old—she was torn from my arms and thrown from the train by an angered guard. I tried to throw myself after her—but I was dragged back into the car. I wanted to die until I came to Terezin and found thousands of children waiting for me—and then I knew I must not die... Do you understand? *(RAJA and HONZA have listened, stunned but calm.)* You are no longer children—and so I tell you. I have a child, and she lives whenever I comfort another child or dry her tears. *(She puts an arm around each of them.)* So, you see, I do have a family. More than anyone else here. *(RAJA and HONZA each put an arm around her. After a moment, she breaks away from them.)* Now, I need your help. Both of you. The children are ready for more than writing, drawing and painting. They need a group project. And I have an idea. Come. I will tell you what I have in mind. *(They exit.)*

(Several CHILDREN, wearing makeshift costumes—representing peasants—dart back and forth across the stage, entering and exiting.)

CHILDREN. Has anyone seen my kerchief?... Does anyone have a pin? My costume keeps falling down... At the end, do we bow two times or three?... Three... Do we chase Honza after we sing, or before?... After. And don't call him Honza. He's Ludvik now... And remember what Irena said—we don't catch him till he's offstage.

(Continued chattering and crossing until RAJA enters.)

RAJA. Hurry along. You must get ready. The audience from the barrack next door will be here soon. *(The CHILDREN exit. RAJA addresses the audience as the musical introduction to "Ludvik" begins.)* Irena had added a new dimension to the children's activities—an operetta, *Ludvik*. Irena was able to enlist the services of several professional musicians who had brought their musical instruments with them when they were shipped to Terezin... The operetta was a full hour long. The story was an old one—the legend of the birds of Cheb and the villain, Ludvik the Carpenter, who hated them because of their singing.

(Offstage whistles and tweets of birds are heard. HONZA, as LUDVIK, enters holding his ears.)

LUDVIK. I can stand it no longer. Those infernal birds are driving me insane!... I know what I shall do. *(He exits.)*

RAJA. He then began to build boxes and cages for the birds. *(Offstage hammering and the sound of laughter is heard from LUDVIK.)*

LUDVICK'S VOICE *(from offstage)*. Now I'll get them!

RAJA. Going into the woods, he trapped the birds one by one. *(The whistles and tweets begin to die down.)*

LUDVIK'S VOICE. I got you! And you! And *you*! You can't fly away from me. *(He laughs until the birds are heard no longer.)*

RAJA. Before long, the village of Cheb lay sad and silent without song.

LUDVIK'S VOICE. Finally. Peace at last.

RAJA. But the smallest child in the village, Pepicek, gathered the children together.

(1ST CHILD, as PEPICEK, enters and motions to offstage. The other CHILDREN, as PEASANTS, enter.)

1ST PEASANT. What is it, Pepicek?

PEPICEK. Ludvik has trapped all the birds, and they can no longer sing.

2ND PEASANT. But what can we do about it?

PEPICEK. Each of us? Nothing. Alone we are helpless. But together, we are not afraid of Ludvik—or of anyone. *(ALL agree.)*

RAJA. And with that, they sang out to the wicked bird catcher.

(SONG #11: "LUDVIK")

PEPICEK & PEASANTS *(singing)*.
> LUDVIK, THE CARPENTER, WARNING WE BRING YOU.
> CHILDREN OF CHEB COME TO CLAIM STOLEN SONG.
> CLOSE BOTH YOUR EARS WHILE OUR MERRY SONGS SING YOU.
> MARCHING TOGETHER WE'LL DRIVE YOU ALONG.
> OUT OF OUR VILLAGE WE'LL RUN YOU AND ROUT YOU,
> FREEING OUR BIRDS FROM YOUR CAGES AND BARS.
> CHILDREN TOGETHER WE DON'T FEAR TO FLOUT YOU,
> STANDING TOGETHER THE VICT'RY IS OURS.

(They exit into the "woods" shouting enthusiastically.)

RAJA *(speaking)*. The children then ran into the woods, freeing the birds, and routing the villain.

(The PEASANTS chase LUDVIK onto the stage, around it, and then back off again. This action is repeated once or twice more as the sound of bird whistles and tweets are heard again. The final time the PEASANTS chase LUDVIK offstage, they stop on stage and listen to the birds sing.)

Act II I NEVER SAW ANOTHER BUTTERFLY

PEASANTS *(GROUP 1, singing)*.
    OUT OF OUR VILLAGE WE ROUTED AND CHASED HIM, FREEING OUR BIRDS FROM HIS CAGES AND BARS. CHILDREN TOGETHER WE STEADFASTLY FACED HIM, STANDING TOGETHER THE VICT'RY WAS OURS.

PEASANTS *(GROUP 2)*.
    AH...

ALL.
    STANDING TOGETHER THE VICT'RY WAS OURS.

(The ringing of bells and continued singing of birds are heard as the PEASANTS exit. The ringing and singing fade.)

RAJA. *Ludvik*—with the rehearsals, the performances—was our hope. We could not let it die. Though the transports continued to carry away children, new children took their places. But *Ludvik* stayed, and the children found strength and courage in playing their parts. *(She exits.)*

(A moment later, the CHILDREN reenter and take deep bows to offstage applause. HONZA enters and bows to the boos of the CHILDREN. He feigns anger and chases them about the stage. Suddenly they stop, then laugh, and ALL hold hands for one final bow. The CHILDREN exit, chattering excitedly as RENKA, RAJA and IRENA enter.)

RENKA. Honza, you were a wonderful villain.

HONZA. I simply imitated the Nazis, that's all. *(They laugh.)*

IRENA. Raja, you did very well with the younger children. They were at the right place every time.

RAJA. I told them if they didn't cooperate, I'd have Honza sit on them. *(More laughter.)*

RENKA. Speaking of the children, I'll make sure they put away their costumes for the next group to use.

HONZA. And I'll get the props back where they belong.

(He and RENKA exit. IRENA notices RAJA looking affectionately at HONZA as he leaves.)

IRENA *(to RAJA)*. You seem to have an interest in our—"villain."

RAJA. Perhaps…a little.

IRENA. A little?

RAJA *(fully confessing)*. Oh, Irena, if he hadn't come back from that project…

IRENA. What would you have done if he had not come back?

RAJA. Waited…and held my breath…for tomorrow…then waited again.

IRENA. You should learn to stop thinking of tomorrow. Keep alive today. That's the secret of waiting—remember that—to keep alive today. Each day—find a reason. Then you will survive.

RAJA. As you have done?

IRENA. Yes. Somehow—one of us is sure to survive. One of us must teach the children how to sing again, to write on paper with a pencil, draw pictures. So we survive each today…

Act II I NEVER SAW ANOTHER BUTTERFLY

RAJA. Yes.

IRENA *(after a moment)*. Now let's go tell the children how wonderful they were. We must always do that, because they always are. *(IRENA puts her arm around RAJA, as they exit.)*

(Moments later the two SOLDIERS enter, each holding a list. A train is heard approaching in the distance. The SOLDIERS call out to an unseen crowd.)

1ST SOLDIER. That completes the names of the adults scheduled for today's transport to Auschwitz.

2ND SOLDIER. Be ready to depart within the hour.

1ST SOLDIER. Next, those under the age of eighteen. *(Reading from his list.)* Eva Heska, Ela Hellrova.

2ND SOLDIER *(reading from his list)*. Petr Fiscal, Marika Friedmanova.

1ST SOLDIER. Frantisek Bass, Bedrick Hoffman. *(The train becomes louder.)*

2ND SOLDIER. Josef Pollack, Dita Valentilcova.

1ST SOLDIER. Nina Ledererova. Eva Steinova. *(The train becomes quite loud.)*

2ND SOLDIER. Hana Lissanova…

1ST SOLDIER. Honza Kosec…

(The shrill whistle of the train pierces the air as the SOLDIERS exit and the lights dim to shadows. An offstage wail of "Noooo!" coming from RAJA is heard almost simultaneously with the train whistle. RAJA enters quickly, searching about frantically.)

RAJA. Honza?… Honza?…

HONZA'S VOICE *(from just offstage)*. Raja...don't—don't turn or move.

RAJA *(trying to locate the voice)*. Honza, where are you?

HONZA. Don't move. Here, on the other side of the wall—don't move, don't—just listen. I have a number in this transport.

RAJA. I know. I heard. *(She searches the darkness for him, moving on hands and knees.)*

HONZA. Please—don't turn, don't move. You know the new rules. If they catch us together, they might put *you* on the transport, too—or worse.

RAJA. What could they do to me that's worse than this. I am losing you.

HONZA. Maybe not. There is good news.

RAJA. What do you mean?

HONZA. The war is coming to an end...

RAJA. Honza... No!

HONZA. Things are going bad for the Nazis—something will happen before long... Raja, please, listen...

RAJA. Honza... Where are you... I'm coming with you.

HONZA. You can't... Irena and Renka—they need you. You must stay with them.

2ND SOLDIER'S VOICE *(from offstage, calling)*. It sounded like it was coming from over here. I'll check.

(Music starts. He enters and sees RAJA. He aims his rifle at her. She recoils, covering her face with her arms. After a long moment, the SOLDIER slowly lowers his rifle. RAJA steals a quick glance in the direction of HONZA which is noticed by the SOLDIER. He crosses to the edge of the stage, again raising his rifle into firing position.

Act II   I NEVER SAW ANOTHER BUTTERFLY

RAJA *(in a trembling whisper)*. No... Please...

(The SOLDIER looks back at RAJA, then to the unseen HONZA, and slowly lowers the rifle.)

1ST SOLDIER'S VOICE *(from offstage)*. Kurt, do you see anything?

2ND SOLDIER *(after a moment, calling to offstage)*. No, Rolf. Nothing. Nothing at all. *(He exits as RAJA almost collapses in relief.)*

(HONZA cautiously emerges from his hiding place.)

HONZA. Raja, I must go now. And you must return to the barrack.

RAJA. I know.

HONZA. Remember, I am with you wherever you go.

RAJA. I know. *(They slowly begin to back away from each other, gazing into each other's eyes.)* Wait. *(They stop.)* Remember when we met—and you told me I didn't know the first thing about anything?

HONZA *(smiling)*. I was wrong.

RAJA. For the most part...perhaps. But there *was* one thing I didn't know the first thing about. And that's the happiness I could know being with someone like you.

(SONG #12: "REPRISE: YOU DON'T KNOW...")

RAJA *(singing)*.
   **I AM A GIRL, AND I KNOW FOR THE FIRST
   TIME WHAT LOVE CAN BE.**

HONZA.
> YOU ARE A GIRL, AND YOU KNOW HOW MUCH
> YOU HAVE MEANT TO ME.

RAJA.
> YOU MADE ME GLAD TO BE ALIVE
> AND SEE THE SUN RISE EV'RY DAY.

HONZA.
> AND YOU BECAME THE SAME TO ME.

BOTH.
> EV'RY DAY FOR YOU I'D PRAY.
> MY HEART WILL ALWAYS BE WITH YOU.

RAJA.
> FOR IT'S TRUE

HONZA.
> YES, IT'S TRUE

RAJA.
> THAT I DO

HONZA.
> AND I, TOO,

RAJA.
> YES, I DO

BOTH.
> BELONG TO YOU,
> BELONG TO YOU!

Act II I NEVER SAW ANOTHER BUTTERFLY   83

(They embrace.)

1ST SOLDIER'S VOICE *(from offstage)*. The transport is loading. All whose names were called must be on it now. *Schnell! Schnell!*

(HONZA and RAJA break their embrace. He starts to leave, then turns back to her. They embrace again and gaze into each other's eyes for a moment. HONZA then exits quickly without looking back.)

RAJA *(staring off into the distance, then slightly above a whisper)*. Goodbye—my love. *(As the sound of a train whistle is heard, she turns to the audience. "Goodbye" underscore begins.)* Goodbye… It should have been the motto of Terezin—written over the entrance. It was goodbye that made us free. It was the only thing we knew would never change. Goodbye… goodbye…goodbye. It freed us all. For what more was there to fear when you had said goodbye to everyone you ever loved? *(She exits.)*

(IRENA enters, ready for transport. She has a shabby jacket over her shoulders and carries a small travel bag. She also has a package of papers wrapped in a shawl and a letter which she has written. She sets the travel bag down and begins to read the letter aloud.)

IRENA. " Raja, Raja Englanderova, you know by now that my number—102866—was called. When you come to school today you will see that I have gone. You will have questions, and I will answer them before you ask. I remember a museum in Prague when I was young. I was fascinated by a room containing medieval paintings, several depicting saints being martyred. But strangely, the saints never seemed to be frightened or in pain. One in particular was about to be pierced by a lance. But he sat there comfortably—as if it had nothing to do with him. Now I understand the saints in the paintings better. What could they do?... I will leave this letter and the last of the pictures and poems, which are wrapped in my shawl, on the school desk. *("Goodbye" underscore ends.)* And remember what they mean to all of us. I have nothing more to give you, so...

(SONG #13: "I LEAVE YOU THESE")

(She sings.)
I LEAVE YOU THESE.
I ASK YOU, PLEASE, TO HIDE THEM WITH THE REST.
AND PRAY THEY MAY BE BLEST.

PERHAPS SOMEDAY THEY WILL BE FOUND
'NEATH THIS SACRED GROUND
ON WHICH THE CHILDREN OF TEREZIN
FOUGHT THEIR FEARS,
TEMPERED THEIR TEARS

WITH THEIR IMAGINATIONS,
PRODUCING THESE PRECIOUS CREATIONS.

IF THEY ARE DISCOVERED,
AFTER THIS WAR IS DONE,

Act II I NEVER SAW ANOTHER BUTTERFLY   85

> **AND THE CHILDREN ARE REMEMBERED,**
> **THEN WE WILL HAVE WON.**
>
> **IF THESE POEMS AND PICTURES**
> **LIVE ON AFTER US ALL,**
> **THEN ON THESE DAYS THE SUN WILL NEVER**
>   **SET,**
> **AND NIGHT SHALL NEVER FALL.**
> **THE WORLD WILL NOT FORGET**
> **THE CHILDREN'S DISTANT CALL.**
> **NIGHT SHALL NEVER FALL.**

(She exits as RENKA enters with the CHILDREN UC where they stand in perhaps a semicircle.)

1ST CHILD *(speaking)*.
   Dawn crawls again across the ghetto streets,
   Embracing all who walk this way.
2ND CHILD.
   Only a car from a long-gone world
   Gobbles up the dark with fiery eyes.
3RD CHILD.
   I've lived in the ghetto for over a year
   In Terezin, the black town now,
4TH CHILD.
   And when I remember my old home so dear,
   I can love it more than I did somehow.

5TH CHILD.
   Sweet remembrance tell a fairy tale
   About my friend who's lost and gone, you see.

6^(TH) CHILD.
>Tell the one about the golden grail,
>And call the swallow, bring her back to me.

7^(TH) CHILD.
>When earth's aflood with morning light,
>A blackbird sings upon a bush

8^(TH) CHILD.
>To greet the dawning after night,
>Then I know how fine it is to live.

(RAJA enters carrying the shawl. She has just read IRENA's note which she folds and puts away.)

RAJA *(singing)*.
>**YES, THEY WERE DISCOVERED**
>**WHEN THE WAR WAS DONE.**

(IRENA enters at the other side of the stage.)

>**THE CHILDREN ARE REMEMBERED.**

RAJA & IRENA.
>**YES, WE HAVE WON.**

>**AND ON THOSE DAYS**
>**THE SUN WILL NEVER SET.**

RAJA.
>**AND NIGHT SHALL NEVER FALL.**

IRENA.
>**THE WORLD WILL NOT FORGET**

Act II I NEVER SAW ANOTHER BUTTERFLY

RAJA.
> **THE CHILDREN'S DISTANT CALL.**

RENKA & IRENA.
> **NIGHT SHALL NEVER FALL.**

(OTHERS enter and join the CHILDREN).

CHILDREN & OTHERS.	RAJA *(speaking)*.
TEREZIN, TEREZIN	My name is Raja…

RENKA & IRENA.
NIGHT SHALL NEVER	I was born in Prague.
FALL	I am a Jew…

CHILDREN & OTHERS.
TEREZIN	I survived Terezin, but more importantly— *(Holding the bundle aloft.)* —so did these.

RENKA, IRENA & GROUP 1.
> **NIGHT SHALL NEVER FALL.**

CURTAIN

CURTAIN CALLS

(SONG #14: "BOWS AND REPRISE: LUDVIK")

(ALL enter in turn and bow.)

CHILDREN *(after the bows, singing)*.
>OUT OF OUR VILLAGE WE ROUTED AND CHASED HIM,
>FREEING OUR BIRDS FROM HIS CAGES AND BARS.
>CHILDREN TOGETHER WE STEADFASTLY FACED HIM,
>STANDING TOGETHER THE VICT'RY WAS OURS.

ALL.
>STANDING TOGETHER THE VICT'RY WAS OURS.

THE END